### KIDS' KITCHEN

# SUGAR
# AND
# SPICE

# SUGAR AND SPICE

WICKEDLY DELICIOUS COOKIES AND
CANDIES FOR JUNIOR CHEFS

**NICOLA FOWLER**

APPLE

A QUINTET BOOK

Published by The Apple Press
6 Blundell Street
London N7 9BH

ISBN 1-85076-626-6

This book was designed and produced by
Quintet Publishing Limited
6 Blundell Street
London N7 9BH

Creative Director: Richard Dewing
Designer: Ian Hunt
Project Editor: Diana Steedman
Editor: Emma Tolkien
Photographer: Jeremy Thomas

Typeset in Great Britain by
Central Southern Typesetters, Eastbourne
Manufactured in Singapore by
Eray Scan Pte Ltd
Printed in Singapore by
Star Standard Industries (Pte) Ltd

ACKNOWLEDGEMENTS

Special thanks to Spencer and Victoria
Dewing, Tom Lolobo, Gee Hyun Kim,
Nick Seruwagi, James and Lucy Stuart, and
to Bob McNiff of the Burlington Junior
School, New Malden, Surrey.

## PUBLISHER'S NOTE

Children should take great care when cooking. Certain techniques such as slicing and chopping or using the stove, oven or grill can be dangerous and extreme care must be exercised at all times. Adults should always supervise while children work in the kitchen.

As far as methods and techniques mentioned in this book are concerned, all statements, information and advice given here are believed to be true and accurate. However, the author, copyright holder, nor the publisher can accept any legal liability for errors or omissions.

# Contents

## 1
### COOKIE KNOW-HOW

## 2
### COOKIE CRAZY

## 3
### SWEET TREATS

## 4
### PERFECT PRESENTS

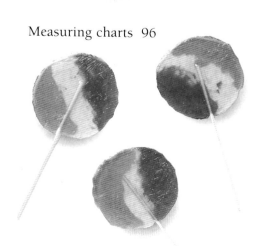

# Introduction

Cooking for the family and friends is lots of fun and *Sugar and Spice* will show you just how easy it can be too. It is never too soon to start learning the simple basics of food preparation and cooking. So, if this is your first attempt, start with the easy recipes first and, when you become more confident, move on to the more involved recipes.

You will find many old favourites together with a selection of unusual and creative ideas. The recipes are easy to follow, with clear step-by-step pictures showing the different techniques required. For safety reasons, some of the photographs are bordered in red, and the instructions are highlighted in bold text. Read Before You Begin first – it is full of important hints and tips – then put on your apron and have fun and enjoy what you are doing.

Happy Cooking

# Before You Begin

Here are a few simple rules you should always follow whenever you are cooking.

Never cook unless there is an adult there to help you. Certain tasks such as chopping with sharp knives, heating liquids and using electrical equipment can be dangerous if not done properly and should always be supervised by an adult. We have highlighted these tasks throughout the book so that you know when to ask for help.

Always read through the recipe before you start and gather together all the ingredients and equipment you will need. Weigh and prepare the ingredients as instructed by the recipe.

All quantities are given in metric and imperial units but make sure that you stick to one system as they are not interchangeable. A useful chart for temperatures, weights and measures is on page 96.

Hygiene is important in the kitchen. Tie your hair back if it is long, wash your hands before touching food and wear an apron to keep your clothes clean.

Keep your working area clean and tidy. Clean up as you go along and have a cloth handy to wipe up spills as soon as they happen.

Be careful not to burn yourself when cooking. Wear oven gloves when handling hot pans, tins and baking sheets and never put your fingers into hot mixtures. If you do accidentally burn yourself, hold the burn under cold water and tell an adult immediately.

Never use electrical equipment near water.

Never leave gas and electric rings on if you have to go out of the kitchen and remember to turn everything off when you have finished.

Finally, always leave the kitchen work surfaces clean and tidy.

# Some Cookery Techniques

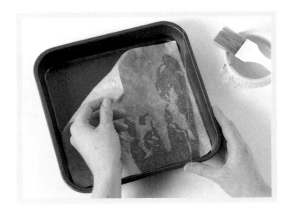

**Knives** must always be used with great care and with an adult present. Never hold the food you are cutting with fingers outstretched; instead, hold the food with your fingertips tucked under and clear of the knife edge. Do not rush and concentrate on what you are doing.

Always **pre-heat the oven** so that it is at the correct temperature throughout the cooking time.

**Greasing and lining tins** prevents cookies and candies from sticking. To grease, put a little vegetable oil on to the tin and spread with a brush, or a piece of kitchen paper, over the base and sides. If the recipe tells you to line the tin, then grease the tin first, place a piece of greaseproof paper in the base and then grease the paper.

## SIFTING FLOUR

**Sifting** flour and icing sugar gets rid of any lumps and helps to make the mixture light and airy.

**Rubbing fat into flour** with your fingertips is a method used in some cookie recipes and in pastry. It is important to keep your fingers cool and to lift the mixture well to add lots of air. It is ready when it looks like breadcrumbs.

## EGGS

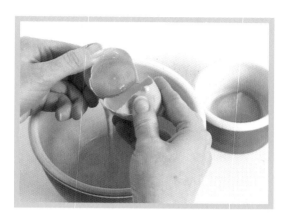 

❚ To **separate an egg** crack firmly against the rim of a small bowl and allow the white to fall into the bowl. You may need to transfer the yolk carefully between the two halves of shell once or twice to allow all the white to fall out. Put the yolk into a separate bowl.

❚ When **adding eggs** to a creamed butter and sugar mixture lightly beat the eggs first, add a little at a time and beat in well after each addition to prevent the mixture from curdling.

## ROLLING AND KNEADING DOUGH

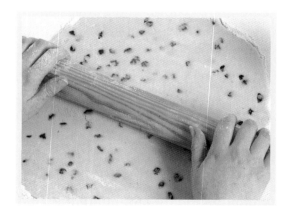 

❚ **Roll dough** on a floured surface with a floured rolling pin to prevent it sticking. Add more flour during the process if necessary.

❚ To **knead** dough, place it on a lightly floured surface and work it between your hands until it is smooth.

▌**Folding** means gently adding ingredients to a mixture which contains a lot of air, for example whisked egg whites. Use a metal spoon and do not beat the mixture.

▌**Melting chocolate** in a bowl over a pan of hot water prevents the chocolate from over-heating and cooking (rather than just melting). Make sure the bowl is big enough to fit over the top of the pan and that the water does not touch the bowl.

▌**Piping** icing and cookie dough is easy with a bit of practise and using a piping bag enables you to control the pressure with your fingers. Experiment with nozzles in different sizes and shapes.

# Safety in the Kitchen

**Heat** Use oven gloves when handling anything that is hot. Never try to take something out of a hot oven without using oven gloves.

▌ When using saucepans, hot dishes or baking tins, use both hands and check first that there is nothing in the way of where you are going to place them once you have removed them from the hob or the oven.

▌ Place hot pans and dishes on a trivet or board. If you feel that a pan or dish is too heavy for you to handle, then ask someone to do it for you.

▌ When on the hob, keep pan handles turned away from you. Angle them to the side and not over the cooker rings which, if turned on, will heat the handles making them too hot to handle.

▌ Do not overfill saucepans as they will then be too heavy to lift. There is also the danger that the contents may boil over if the pan is filled close to the brim.

▌ Call an adult immediately if a fire breaks out. Do NOT try to deal with it yourself.

▌ Do not be tempted to test for heat by placing your hand or fingers on or in anything that may be hot.

▌ Turn off the cooker, microwave and any electrical implements that have been used as soon as you have finished with them.

▌ As well as informing an adult when you are beginning to cook you must also tell them when you have finished so they can check that electrical implements are safely turned off.

# CHAPTER ONE

# Cookie Know-how

# Oat Crunch Cookies

Makes about 18 cookies

## YOU WILL NEED

100g (4oz) unsalted butter,
  cut into pieces
2 level tablespoons golden
  syrup
75g (3oz) light brown
  soft sugar
175g (6oz) plain four, sifted
50g (2oz) porridge oats
1 egg, size 3, lightly beaten

1 **Pre-heat the oven to 150°C/300°F/Gas mark 2.**
Lightly grease two baking sheets.

2 Put the butter and syrup into a medium
saucepan and **melt together over a gentle heat,
stirring occasionally. Remove the pan from the
heat** and place on a heatproof surface.

3 Add all the dry ingredients to the saucepan.
Finally add the egg.

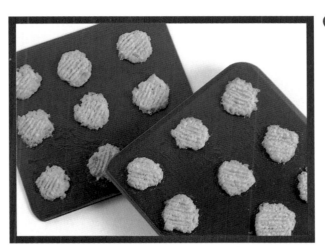

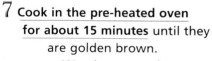

4 Stir the mixture with a wooden spoon until it is well combined.

5 Using two teaspoons, place heaped teaspoons of the mixture on the greased baking sheets. Leave plenty of room between each cookie to allow them to spread during cooking.

6 Press the cookies down with the back of a fork to flatten them slightly.

7 **Cook in the pre-heated oven for about 15 minutes** until they are golden brown. Wearing oven gloves, **remove the baking sheets from the oven** and leave the cookies to cool for five minutes. Then, using a spatula, transfer to a cooling rack and leave until cold.

# Shortbread Shells

Makes 12 cookies

**YOU WILL NEED**

225g (8oz) unsalted butter,
  at room temperature
100g (4oz) caster sugar
  (plus extra for sprinkling)
300g (10oz) plain flour, sifted
50g (2oz) ground rice
pinch salt

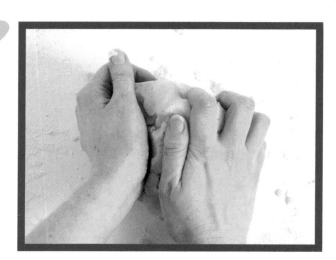

1 **Pre-heat the oven to 200°C/400°F/Gas
mark 6**. In a large bowl, **beat the butter and
sugar together with an electric beater**
until the mixture is creamy and light.

2 With a wooden spoon, beat in
the remaining ingredients until
the mixture is well combined.

3 Turn the dough onto a
surface dusted with flour
and knead lightly until it
is smooth.

4 Divide the mixture into 12 and press the dough into madeleine tins.

5 **Cook in the pre-heated oven for 12 to 15 minutes** until lightly golden. Wearing oven gloves, **remove the tin from the oven** and leave the cookies to cool in the tins for 10 minutes, then carefully turn out onto a cooling rack. When completely cold, sprinkle with a little caster sugar.

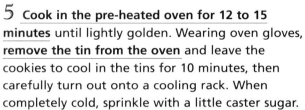

# Fruity Flapjacks

Makes 9 cookies

## YOU WILL NEED

50g (2oz) dried, ready-to-eat
  apricots
50g (2oz) dried, ready-to-eat
  prunes
100g (4oz) unsalted butter, cut
  into pieces
50g (2oz) light brown soft sugar
3 level tablespoons honey
175g (6oz) porridge oats
large pinch salt

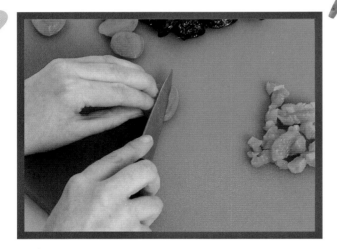

$1$ **Pre-heat the oven to 180°C/350°F/Gas mark 4.**
Grease an 18cm x 18cm (7in x 7in) shallow
tin. Then **using a small knife, cut apricots and
prunes into small pieces** and set aside.

$2$ Put the butter, sugar and honey into a large
saucepan and **melt over a gentle heat, stirring
occasionally.**

$3$ **Remove the pan from the heat** and place on a
heatproof surface. Add the chopped apricots and
prunes, oats and salt to the saucepan.

4 Stir the mixture until well combined.

5 Spoon the mixture into the greased tin and, using the back of a large spoon, press the mixture down firmly until the surface is level.

6 **Cook in the pre-heated oven for 25 minutes.** Wearing oven gloves, **remove the tin from the oven** and leave to cool on a wire rack for 5 minutes. Then **mark into 9 squares with a small, sharp knife** and leave the cookies in the tin until completely cold.

7 When cold, loosen the squares and remove from the tin.

# Nice Spice Cookies

Makes about 25 cookies

## YOU WILL NEED

1 small lemon, skin scrubbed clean

175g (6oz) unsalted butter, at room temperature

75g (3oz) light brown soft sugar

1 egg, size 3, lightly beaten

225g (8oz) plain flour, sifted

2 level teaspoons ground cinnamon

½ level teaspoon ground nutmeg

½ level teaspoon ground ginger

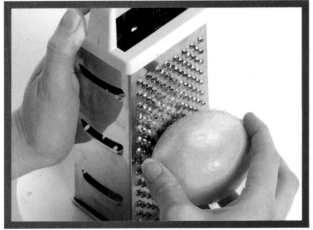

1 **Pre-heat the oven to 180°C/350°F/Gas mark 4.** Lightly grease two baking sheets. Finely grate the rind of the lemon and set aside.

2 In a large bowl, **beat the butter and sugar with an electric beater** until the mixture is creamy and light.

### CHEF'S TIP

☞ Squeeze the juice of the lemon, add a little hot water and sugar. Cool the syrup and then top up with water for a refreshing drink.

3 Then add the egg, a little at a time, **beating well between each addition**. Add the lemon rind.

4 Add the sifted flour and spices and, using a wooden spoon, stir well until the mixture forms a stiff dough.

5 Knead the dough lightly in the bowl and, using your hands, shape the dough into approximately 25 small balls.

6 Place the balls on the greased baking sheets, leaving room between each for spreading during cooking.

7 Make a pattern on the cookies by flattening each slightly with the prongs of a fork dipped in flour in two directions to make a criss-cross pattern. **Cook in the pre-heated oven for about 10 minutes until golden**. Wearing oven gloves, **remove the baking sheets from the oven** and cool on a heatproof surface for five minutes. Then, with a spatula, transfer the cookies to a cooling rack and leave until cold.

# Jewelled Sugar Cookies

Makes about 25 cookies

**YOU WILL NEED**

50g (2oz) unsalted butter,
   at room temperature
100g (4oz) caster sugar
1 egg plus 1 egg yolk, size 3,
   lightly beaten
225g (8oz) plain flour, sifted
½ level teaspoon baking powder
pinch salt
a few drops almond essence
25g (1oz) multi-coloured sugar
   crystals

1 In a large bowl, **beat the butter and sugar with an electric beater** until the mixture is creamy and light.

2 Add the egg, a little at a time, **beating well between each addition**.

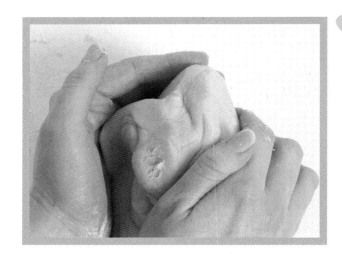

3 Add the flour, baking powder, salt and almond essence and mix with a wooden spoon until well combined.

4 Turn the dough onto a surface dusted with flour and knead lightly until it is smooth. Then wrap the dough in foil or in a plastic bag and refrigerate for 30 minutes.

5 **Pre-heat the oven to 180°C/350°F/Gas mark 4.** Lightly grease two baking sheets. Sprinkle a surface with flour and roll out the dough with a floured rolling pin until it is about 5mm (¼in) thick.

6 Using a heart-shaped cutter, cut cookies out of the dough, lightly re-kneading and re-rolling the dough until it is all used up. Place the cookies on the baking sheets, leaving a little space around each one.

7 Sprinkle the cookies with coloured sugar crystals. **Cook in the pre-heated oven for about 10 minutes until pale golden**. Wearing oven gloves, **remove the baking sheets from the oven**, place on a heatproof surface and leave the cookies to cool for 5 minutes. Then, with a spatula, transfer the cookies to a cooling rack and leave until cold.

# Chocolate Crunch Bars

Makes about 16 bars

**YOU WILL NEED**

225g (8oz) digestive biscuits

100g (4oz) chocolate honeycomb bars

100g (4oz) unsalted butter, cut into pieces

4 level tablespoons golden syrup

100g (4oz) plain chocolate drops

15g (½oz) icing sugar

1 Line the base and sides of a 23cm x 15cm (9in x 6in) dish with a piece of aluminium foil.

2 Put the digestive biscuits and chocolate honeycomb bars into plastic bags and crush coarsely with a rolling pin.

3 Put the butter and syrup into a large saucepan and **melt over a gentle heat, stirring. Remove the pan from the heat** and place on a heatproof surface.

**4**

**5**

**6**

**7**

4 Stir the chocolate drops into the melted butter and syrup until the chocolate has melted and the mixture is smooth.

5 Add the crushed biscuits and chocolate honeycomb to the melted mixture in the saucepan and stir well to combine.

6 Pour the mixture into the prepared dish and smooth the surface with the back of a spoon. Let it cool, and then refrigerate for at least 2 hours.

7 Turn the chilled mixture onto a chopping board, remove the foil and sprinkle with icing sugar. **Cut into bars to serve**.

# Coconut Crisp

Makes about 18 cookies

## YOU WILL NEED

40g (1½oz) plain flour
50g (2oz) unsalted butter,
    at room temperature
100g (4oz) caster sugar
2 egg whites
25g (1oz) dessicated coconut

1 **Pre-heat the oven to
180°C/350°F/Gas mark 4**.
Lightly grease two large baking
sheets. Sift the flour into a bowl.

2 In a separate bowl, **beat the
butter and sugar with an
electric beater** until the mixture
is creamy and light.

3 Add the egg whites to the
butter and sugar and **gently
mix until just combined**.

4 Finally, add the sifted flour and dessicated coconut and mix with a spoon.

5 Put heaped teaspoons of the mixture onto the prepared baking sheets, leaving plenty of room for spreading.

6 **Cook in the pre-heated oven for about 8 minutes** until the cookies are brown around the edges.

7 Wearing oven gloves, **remove the baking sheets from the oven**, place on a heatproof surface and leave the cookies to cool on the baking sheets for 5 minutes. Then, with a spatula, transfer the cookies to a wire rack to cool completely.

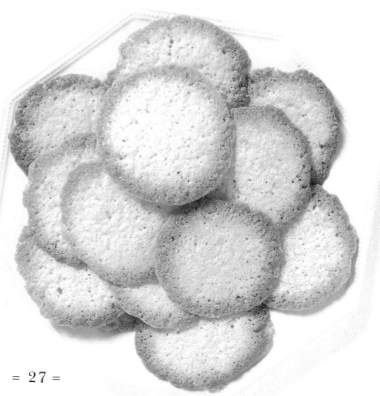

# Fruit 'n' Nut Brownies

Makes about 16 cookies

## YOU WILL NEED

75g (3oz) plain chocolate,
  broken into small pieces
75g (3oz) butter, at room
  temperature
175g (6oz) caster sugar
3 eggs, size 3, lightly beaten
1 teaspoon vanilla essence
75g (3oz) self-raising flour,
  sifted
pinch salt
50g (2oz) walnuts, chopped
50g (2oz) raisins

1 **Pre-heat the oven to 180°C/350°F/Gas mark 4.** Grease, line base and grease base of a 20cm x 20cm (8in x 8in) shallow tin

2 Half fill a medium-sized saucepan with water and **bring to the boil. Take the saucepan off the heat** and place on a heatproof surface. Place the chocolate in a bowl that will sit on top of the saucepan without touching the water. Put the bowl on top of the pan and stir the chocolate occasionally until it has melted and is smooth.

3 Meanwhile, put the butter and sugar into a separate large bowl and **beat with an electric beater** until the mixture is creamy and light. Add the egg, a little at a time, **beating well between each addition**.

4 Add all the remaining ingredients, except the melted chocolate, and stir well to combine.

5 Finally, add the melted chocolate and stir until well mixed.

6 Spoon the mixture into the prepared tin and **cook in the pre-heated oven for approximately 25 minutes**.

7 Wearing oven gloves, **remove the tin from the oven** and place on a cooling rack. Leave the brownies in the tin to cool and then **cut into squares**.

## CHEF'S TIP

☞ Brownies should be soft and chewy in the middle, so be careful not to let them overcook and become dry.

# Blueberry Biscuits

Makes about 20

## YOU WILL NEED

175g (6oz) unsalted butter,
   at room temperature
100g (4oz) caster sugar
1 egg, size 3, lightly beaten
1 teaspoon vanilla essence
225g (8oz) self-raising flour,
   sifted
50g (2oz) dried blueberries

1 In a large bowl, **beat the butter and sugar with an electric beater** until the mixture is creamy and light.

2 Add the egg, a little at a time, **beating well between each addition.**

3 Add the vanilla essence and then the flour, mixing with a spoon until well combined.

4 Stir in the blueberries.

5 Turn the dough onto a surface dusted with flour and knead lightly until it is smooth. Form the dough into a round, wrap and refrigerate for 30 minutes.

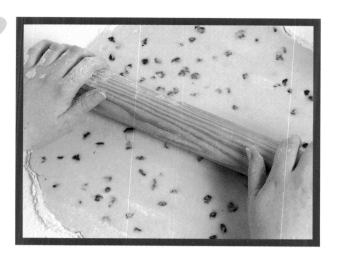

6 **Pre-heat the oven to 180°C/350°F/Gas mark 4**. Lightly grease two baking sheets. Sprinkle a little flour on a surface and roll out the chilled dough with a floured rolling pin until it is about 5mm (¼in) thick.

7 Cut out cookies using a crinkly-edged round cookie cutter. Lightly re-knead and re-roll the dough until it is all used up. Place the cookies on the prepared baking sheet and **cook in the pre-heated oven for about 15 minutes until golden.** Wearing oven gloves, **remove the baking sheets from the oven**, place on a heatproof surface and leave the cookies to cool for 5 minutes. Then, with a spatula, transfer the cookies to a cooling rack and leave to cool completely.

# Peanut Butter Cookies

Makes about 16

## YOU WILL NEED

50g (2oz) unsalted butter, at
    room temperature
100g (4oz) crunchy peanut
    butter
175g (6oz) light brown soft
    sugar
1 egg, size 3, lightly beaten
1 teaspoon vanilla essence
225g (8oz) plain flour, sifted
1 level teaspoon baking powder
pinch of salt
16 unsalted and blanched
    peanuts

1 **Pre-heat the oven to
180°C/350°F/Gas mark 4.**
Grease two baking sheets. In a
large bowl, **cream together the
butter and peanut butter with
an electric beater.**

2 Add the sugar and continue
to **beat until the mixture is
creamy and light.**

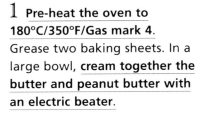

$3$ Add the egg, a little at a time, **beating well between each addition.**

$4$ Now add all the remaining ingredients, except the peanuts, mix well with a spoon and form into a ball.

$5$ Turn the dough onto a surface dusted with flour and knead lightly until it is smooth. Sprinkle the surface with flour again and roll out the dough with a floured rolling pin until it is about 5mm (¼in) thick.

6 Cut the dough into rounds using a plain round cutter. Lightly re-knead and re-roll dough until it is all used up.

7 Put the cookies on the prepared baking sheets and place a peanut in the centre of each cookie. **Cook in the pre-heated oven for about 10 minutes until golden.** Wearing oven gloves, **remove the baking sheets from the oven**, place on a heatproof surface and leave the cookies to cool for 5 minutes. Then, with a spatula, transfer the cookies to a cooling rack and leave until cold.

# Giant Double Choc Chip Cookies

Makes 8 cookies

**YOU WILL NEED**

225g (8oz) unsalted butter,
   at room temperature
225g (8oz) caster sugar
1 egg, size 3, lightly beaten
300g (10oz) self-raising flour,
   sifted
25g (1oz) cocoa, sifted
pinch salt
100g (4oz) white chocolate
   drops

1 **Pre-heat the oven to 180°C/350°F/Gas mark 4.** Lightly grease two large baking sheets. In a large bowl, **beat the butter and sugar with an electric beater** until the mixture is creamy and light.

2 Add the egg, a little at a time, **beating well between each addition**.

3 Add the remaining ingredients and mix well with a spoon to combine.

4 Turn the dough onto a surface dusted with flour and knead lightly until it is smooth.

5 Form the dough into eight equal balls.

6 Lightly flour the surface again and roll each ball into a flat cookie with a floured rolling pin until each cookie is about 13cm (5in) in diameter.

7 Place the cookies on the prepared baking sheets and **cook in the pre-heated oven for about 12 minutes.**

8 Wearing oven gloves, **remove the baking sheets from the oven**, place on a heatproof surface and leave the cookies to cool for 10 minutes. Then, with a spatula, transfer the cookies to a wire rack to cool completely.

## CHEF'S TIP

☞ You could make smaller cookies by following the recipe to Step 4, then rolling the dough and cutting with a cookie cutter. They may need a little less cooking time.

# Fast Freezer Cookies

Makes about 25 cookies

## YOU WILL NEED

175g (6oz) butter, at room
  temperature
225g (8oz) caster sugar
1 egg, size 3, lightly beaten
50g (2oz) ground almonds
175g (6oz) self-raising flour,
  sifted
pinch salt

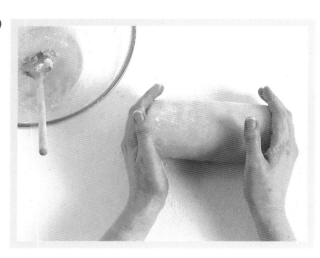

1 In a large bowl, **beat the butter and sugar with an electric beater** until the mixture is creamy and light. Add the egg, a little at a time, **beating well between each addition**.

2 Add all the remaining ingredients and beat well with a spoon.

3 Shape the dough into a roll. It will be very soft.

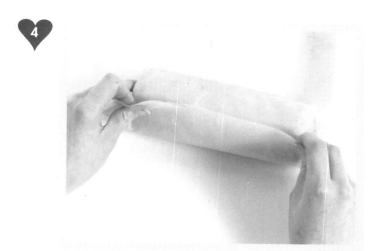

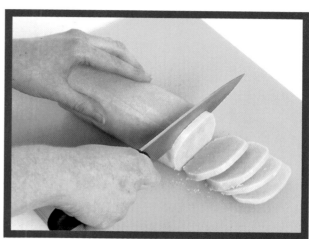

4 Wrap the dough roll in greaseproof paper and put into the freezer until you want to bake the cookies.

5 Take the dough out of the freezer 10 minutes before you want to bake the cookies. **Pre-heat the oven to 200°C/ 400°F/Gas mark 6** and grease a baking sheet. **Slice the required number of cookies – about 5mm (¼in) thick – from the roll using a sharp knife.**

6 Place the cookies on the greased baking sheet. Do not worry if they are a bit curly and do not sit flat on the sheet. They will flatten out in the oven.

7 **Cook in the pre-heated oven for about 9 minutes** until golden brown. Wearing oven gloves, **remove the baking sheet from the oven**, place on a heatproof surface and leave the cookies to cool on the sheet for 5 minutes. With a spatula, transfer to a wire rack to cool completely.

# CHAPTER TWO

# Cookie Crazy

# Animal Farm Gingerbread

Makes about 35 small cookies

## YOU WILL NEED

100g (4oz) unsalted butter, cut
  into pieces
100g (4oz) light brown soft
  sugar
1 level tablespoon golden syrup
225g (8oz) plain flour
1 level teaspoon baking powder
2 level teaspoons ground ginger
225g (8oz) icing sugar, sifted
8–12 teaspoons hot water
pink and yellow food colouring

1 Put the butter, sugar and syrup into a large saucepan and **melt over a gentle heat, stirring. Remove the pan from the heat**, place on a heatproof surface and allow the mixture to cool for 10 minutes.

2 Sift the flour, baking powder and ginger together and add to the saucepan. Mix well and form the dough into a ball. Wrap the dough and refrigerate for 30 minutes.

it is all used up. **Cook in the pre-heated oven for 7–8 minutes until golden.** Wearing oven gloves, **remove the baking sheets from the oven**, place on a heatproof surface and leave the cookies to cool for 5 minutes. Then, with a spatula, transfer the cookies to a wire rack and leave until cold.

5 Meanwhile, put the icing sugar into a bowl. Add about half the water and mix well. Then continue adding more water, a teaspoon at a time, stirring well after each addition, until you achieve a fairly thick icing that will hold its shape when piped.

3 **Pre-heat the oven to 180°C/350°F/Gas mark 4.** Lightly grease two baking sheets. On a lightly floured surface, roll out the chilled dough with a floured rolling pin until it is about 5mm (¼in) thick.

4 Using animal shaped cookie cutters, cut shapes from the dough and place on the prepared baking sheets. Lightly re-knead and re-roll the dough until

6 Divide the icing up into small bowls, leave one white and colour each of the others a different colour with a few drops of food colouring, eg pink for pigs, yellow for chicks.

7 Using one colour at a time, put the icing into a piping bag fitted with a plain writing nozzle. Cover the remaining bowls of icing with a damp cloth until you are ready to use them. Pipe faces and patterns onto the cookies and leave to dry before serving.

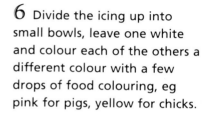

**CHEF'S TIP**

 You can buy a variety of animal shaped cookie cutters from kitchen shops, supermarkets and department stores.

# Cookie Crumbles

Makes about 16 cookies

## YOU WILL NEED

150g (5oz) unsalted butter,
   at room temperature
50g (2oz) caster sugar
200g (7oz) plain flour, sifted
25g (1oz) cornflour
75g (3oz) jam
50g (2oz) light brown soft sugar

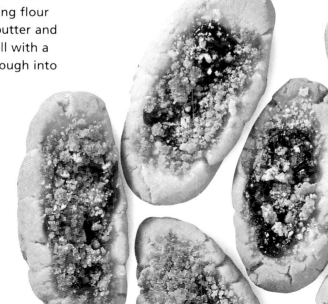

1 **Pre-heat the oven to 180°C/ 350°F/Gas mark 4**. Grease two baking sheets. Put aside 25g (1oz) of the butter. Put the remaining butter into a large bowl and **beat with an electric beater until soft**. Add the caster sugar and **beat again** until the mixture is creamy and light.

2 Put aside 50g (2oz) of the flour. Add the remaining flour and cornflour to the butter and sugar mixture, mix well with a spoon and form the dough into a ball.

3 Take small pieces of the dough and roll into fingers. Place each on the baking sheets, allowing room for spreading during cooking. With your finger, make a small indent down the centre of each cookie.

4 Fill the indent with a little jam.

5 Now make the crumble topping. Put the reserved butter and flour into a bowl and rub together with your fingers until the mixture looks like breadcrumbs. Stir in the brown sugar.

6 Sprinkle the crumble topping over the cookies. **Cook in the pre-heated oven for about 15 minutes.** Wearing oven gloves, **remove the baking sheets from the oven,** place on

a heatproof surface and leave the cookies to cool for 10 minutes. With a spatula, transfer the cookies to a cooling rack and leave until cold.

### CHEF'S TIP

☞ This is a good recipe for using up little bits of jam left in the bottom of the jar. Try different flavours in each cookie.

# Ice Cream Sandwiches

Makes about 18

## YOU WILL NEED

100g (4oz) unsalted butter, at room temperature

175g (6oz) caster sugar

1 egg, size 3, lightly beaten

225g (8oz) self-raising flour, sifted

½ litre (1 pint) ice-cream, any flavour

1 In a large bowl, **beat the butter and sugar with an electric beater** until the mixture is creamy and light. Add the egg, a little at a time, **beating well** between each addition.

2 Add the sifted flour, mix well with a spoon and form the dough into a ball. Cover and refrigerate for about 30 minutes.

3 **Pre-heat the oven to 180°C/350°F/Gas mark 4.** Lightly grease two baking sheets. On a floured surface, knead the chilled dough lightly and roll out with a floured rolling pin until the dough measures about 30mm x 30mm (12in x 12in).

**4**

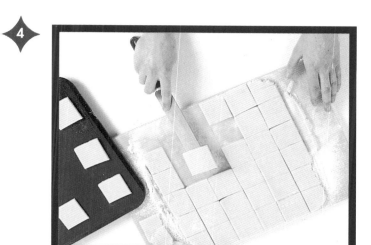

**5**

**6**

$4$ **Using a sharp knife, cut the dough into strips at 5mm (2in) intervals. Then cut across the strips at 5mm (2in) intervals so that you have 36 squares.** With a palette knife, lift the squares and place on the prepared baking sheets, leaving room for spreading.

$5$ **Cook in the pre-heated oven for about 10 minutes until golden.** Wearing oven gloves, **remove the baking sheets from the oven**, place on a heatproof surface and leave the cookies to cool for 10 minutes. Then, with a spatula, transfer the cookies to a wire rack to cool completely.

$6$ When the cookies are cold, remove the ice-cream from the freezer and allow to stand for five minutes at room temperature. Then spoon ice-cream on to half of the cookies, **pushing it down with a knife** to give a flat surface. Place a cookie on top of the ice-cream to make a "sandwich".

# Twinkle Stars

Makes about 20 cookies

## YOU WILL NEED

175g (6oz) unsalted butter,
  at room temperature
225g (8oz) self-raising flour,
  sifted
50g (2oz) light brown soft sugar
½ teaspoon vanilla essence
pinch salt
edible silver sugar balls
edible silver powder

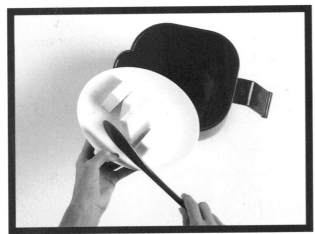

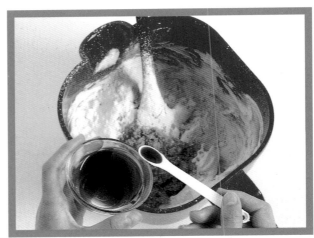

1 **Pre-heat the oven to 190°C/375°F/Gas mark 5.** Lightly grease two baking sheets. Place the butter in a bowl and beat with a wooden spoon until soft.

2 Sift the flour into the bowl, then add the sugar, vanilla essence and salt. Mix well. The dough will be crumbly so roll it into a ball with your hands. Transfer to a lightly floured surface. Knead lightly until smooth.

3 Roll out the dough with a floured rolling pin until it is about 5mm (¼in) thick.

5 Press a silver sugar ball onto each point of the stars. **Cook in the pre-heated oven for 13–15 minutes until the cookies are golden.** Wearing oven gloves, **remove the baking sheets from the oven,** place on a heatproof surface and leave the cookies to cool for 5 minutes. Then, with a spatula, transfer the cookies to a cooling rack and leave until cold.

6 Use a clean paintbrush to paint carefully the outline of the cookies with a thin coat of silver dust.

4 Cut out cookies using a star-shaped cookie cutter. Using a spatula, transfer to a baking sheet. Lightly re-knead and re-roll dough until it is all used up.

# Alpha-Biccies

Makes about 20 letters

## YOU WILL NEED

100g (4oz) unsalted butter,
  cut into pieces
225g (8oz) plain flour, sifted
100g (4oz) caster sugar
1 level tablespoon poppy seeds
1 egg, size 3, lightly beaten
few drops of vanilla essence
175g (6oz) icing sugar, sifted
6–8 teaspoons hot water
25g (1oz) hundreds and
  thousands

1 **Pre-heat the oven to 200°C/400°F/Gas mark 6.**
Lightly grease two baking sheets. Put the butter
and flour into a large bowl and rub the butter into
the flour with your fingertips until the mixture
looks like breadcrumbs.

2 Stir in the sugar and poppy seeds, followed by
the egg and vanilla essence.

3 Form the dough into a ball, turn onto a lightly
floured surface and knead the dough lightly.

**4**

**5**

**6**

Then, with a spatula, transfer the cookies to a wire rack and leave until cold. Meanwhile, put the icing sugar into a bowl, add about half the water and mix well. Then continue adding more water, a teaspoon at a time, stirring well after each addition, until you achieve a thick icing that will spread.

6 With a small palette knife, spread the icing on the cookies. If necessary, dip the palette knife in hot water from time to time to make the spreading easier. While the icing is still wet, sprinkle the cookies with hundreds and thousands and leave to dry.

4 Sprinkle the surface with flour again and roll out the dough with a floured rolling pin until it is about 5mm (¼in) thick. Using letter-shaped cookie cutters or cardboard templates and a sharp knife, **cut out letters from the rolled dough**.

5 Put the cookies carefully onto the prepared baking sheets and **cook for about 10 minutes until golden**. Wearing oven gloves, **remove the baking sheets from the oven**, place on a heatproof surface and leave the cookies to cool for 5 minutes.

# Wriggly Worms

Makes about 10 cookies

## YOU WILL NEED

100g (4oz) unsalted butter,
  at room temperature
50g (2oz) icing sugar, sifted
1 egg, size 3, lightly beaten
175g (6oz) plain flour, sifted
175g (6oz) icing sugar, sifted
6–8 teaspoons hot water
few drops of pink food
  colouring

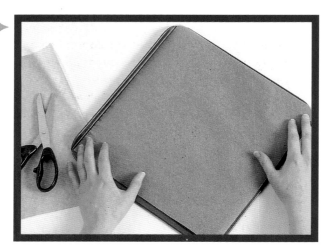

$1$ **Pre-heat the oven to 180°C/350°F/Gas mark 4**.
Line a baking sheet with parchment paper.

$2$ In a large bowl, **beat the butter and 50g (2oz) of the icing sugar with an electric beater** until the mixture is creamy and light. Add the egg, a little at a time, beating well between each addition.

$3$ Add the flour and mix well with a spoon.

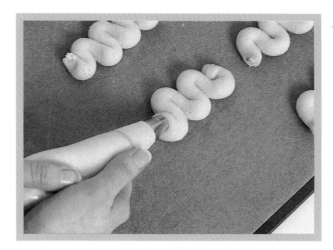

4 Spoon the cookie mixture into a large piping bag fitted with a 1cm (½in) plain nozzle.

5 Pipe about 10 wriggly shapes onto the parchment paper leaving space for spreading.

6 **Cook in the pre-heated oven for approximately 10 minutes** until golden. Wearing oven gloves, **remove the baking sheet from the oven**, place on a heatproof surface and leave the cookies to cool for 5 minutes. Then, with a spatula, transfer the cookies to a cooling rack and leave until cold.

7 Meanwhile, make the icing. Put the remaining icing sugar into a bowl, add about half the water and mix well. Then continue adding more water, a teaspoon at a time, stirring well after each addition, until you achieve a thick icing that will hold its shape when piped. Add a few drops of food colouring and put the icing in a small piping bag fitted with a plain writing nozzle. Pipe eyes and a zig-zag pattern onto each "worm". Leave to dry before serving.

### CHEF'S TIP

☞ Place a piping bag in a small bowl or wide glass and fold the sides over the edge to support the bag while you fill it.

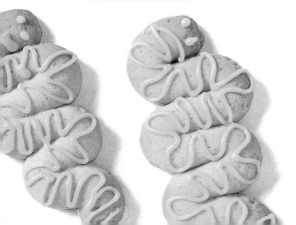

# Christmas Cookies

Makes about 35 cookies

**YOU WILL NEED**

50g (2oz) unsalted butter,
  at room temperature
100g (4oz) light brown soft
  sugar
1 egg plus 1 egg yolk, size 3,
  lightly beaten
225g (8oz) plain flour, sifted
½ level teaspoon baking powder
pinch salt
2 level teaspoons mixed spice
225g (8oz) icing sugar, sifted
8–12 teaspoons hot water
yellow, green and red food
  colouring
fine coloured ribbon or string

1 In a large bowl, **beat the butter and sugar with an electric beater** until the mixture is creamy and light. Add the egg, a little at a time, **beating well** between each addition.

2 Add the flour, baking powder, salt and mixed spice and mix with a wooden spoon until well combined. Turn the dough onto a surface dusted with flour and knead lightly until it is smooth. Then wrap the dough in foil or in a plastic bag and refrigerate for 30 minutes.

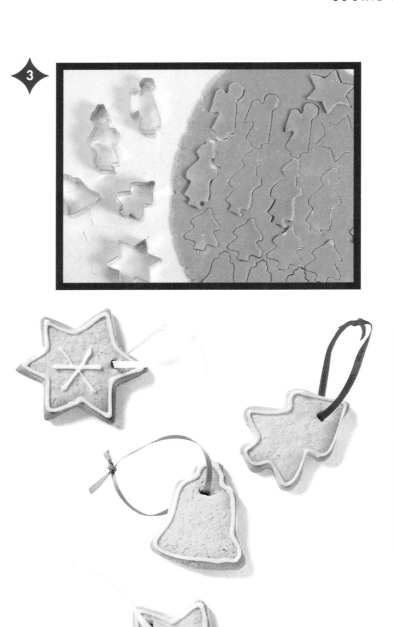

3 **Pre-heat the oven to 180°C/350°F/Gas mark 4.** Lightly grease two baking sheets. Sprinkle a surface with flour and roll out the dough with a floured rolling pin until it is about 5mm (¼in) thick. Using Christmas cookie cutters, cut cookies out of the dough, lightly re-kneading and re-rolling the dough until it is all used up.

4 With a cocktail stick make a little hole at the top of each cookie. Place them on the baking sheets, leaving a little space around each one.

5 **Cook in the pre-heated oven for about 10 minutes** until golden. Wearing oven gloves, **remove the baking sheets from the oven**, place on a heatproof surface and leave the cookies to cool for 5 minutes. Then, with a spatula, transfer the cookies to a cooling rack and leave until cold.

6

7

6 Meanwhile, put the icing sugar into a bowl, add about half the water and mix well. Then continue adding more water, a teaspoon at a time, stirring well after each addition, until you achieve a thick icing that will hold its shape when piped. Divide the icing up into small bowls, leave one white and colour each of the others a different colour with a few drops of food colouring, e.g. yellow, green and red. Using one colour at a time, put the icing into a piping bag fitted with a plain writing nozzle. Cover the remaining bowls of icing with a damp cloth until you are ready to use them. Pipe outlines and patterns onto the cookies.

7 When the icing has dried, thread a piece of coloured ribbon through the hole in each cookie, tie in a bow and use to hang the cookies on the Christmas tree.

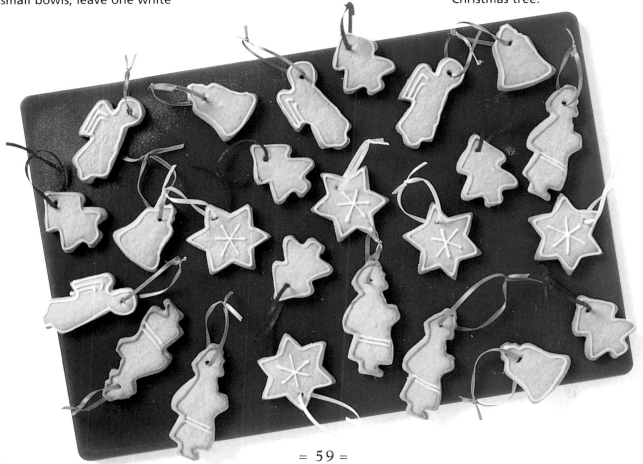

# Crazy Faces

Makes about 20 cookies

## YOU WILL NEED

50g (2oz) unsalted butter,
  at room temperature
100g (4oz) caster sugar
1 egg plus 1 egg yolk, size 3,
  lightly beaten
225g (8oz) plain flour, sifted
½ level teaspoon baking powder
pinch salt
½ teaspoon vanilla essence
ready-to-roll icing in assorted
  colours

1 **Pre-heat the oven to 180°C/350°F/Gas mark 4**.
Lightly grease two baking sheets. In a large bowl,
**beat the butter and sugar with an electric beater**
until the mixture is creamy and light. Add the egg,
a little at a time, **beating well between each
addition**. Add the flour, baking powder, salt and
vanilla essence and stir with a spoon until well
combined.

2 Turn the dough onto a surface dusted with
flour and knead lightly until it is smooth. Sprinkle
the surface with flour again and roll out the
dough with a floured rolling pin until it is about
5mm (¼in) thick. Cut out cookies with a plain
round cookie cutter and place them on the
prepared baking sheets. Lightly re-knead and re-
roll the dough until it is all used up.

**3**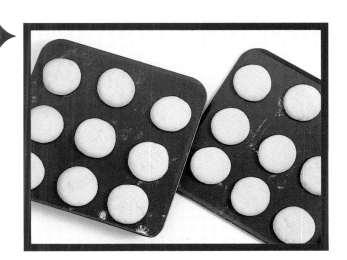

**4**

**5**

**6**

3 **Cook in the pre-heated oven for about 10 minutes** until they are lightly browned. Wearing oven gloves, **remove the baking sheets from the oven**, place on a heatproof surface and leave the cookies to cool for 5 minutes. Then, with a spatula, transfer the cookies to a cooling rack and leave until cold.

4 Meanwhile, lightly dust a surface with icing sugar and roll out each colour of the ready-to-roll icing.

5 Using cookie cutters, aspic cutters and/or a small knife, **cut out shapes** from the ready-to-roll icing to make faces.

6 Dampen the underside of the icing slightly with water to stick the icing to the cookies.

# Butterfly Whirls

Makes about 10 cookies

**YOU WILL NEED**

175g (6oz) unsalted butter,
    at room temperature
225g (8oz) self-raising flour,
    sifted
50g (2oz) light brown soft sugar
½ teaspoon vanilla essence
pinch of salt
green food colouring
5 liquorice strands

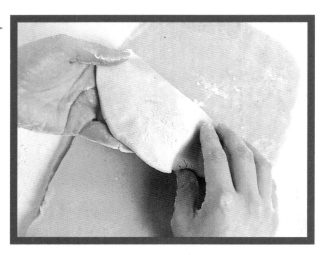

1 **Pre-heat the oven to 190°C/375°F/Gas mark 5.** Lightly grease two baking sheets. Put the butter into a bowl and beat with a wooden spoon until soft. Add the flour, sugar, vanilla essence and salt and mix well. Form the dough into a ball and knead on a lightly floured surface until smooth. Divide the dough in two.

2 Add a few drops of green food colouring to one half of the dough and knead well until the colour is evenly mixed in.

3 On a floured surface, roll each piece of dough with a floured rolling pin until each is approximately 26cm x 13cm (10in x 5in). Place one piece of dough on top of the other.

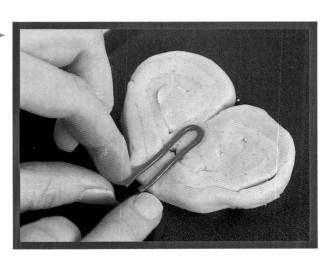

$4$ From one short end, roll up the dough to the middle. Do the same from the other end.

$5$ **With a knife, slice through the roll at 1cm (½in) intervals** and place the cookies on the prepared baking sheets, leaving room for spreading. Press each cookie down lightly with your hand to flatten slightly.

$6$ **Cut the liquorice into 7.5mm (3in) lengths,** fold in half and press one into the middle of each cookie, overlapping the edge, to make the antennae. **Cook in the pre-heated oven for approximately 15 minutes** until golden. Wearing oven gloves, **remove from the oven**, place on a heatproof surface and leave the cookies to cool for 5 minutes. Transfer them to a cooling rack and leave until cold.

# Meringue Mushrooms

*Makes about 20*

**YOU WILL NEED**

2 eggs, size 3
½ teaspoon white wine vinegar
100g (4oz) caster sugar
25g (1oz) unsalted butter
100g (4oz) plain or milk
   chocolate, broken into small
   pieces
1 tablespoon milk

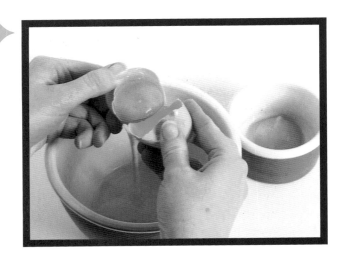

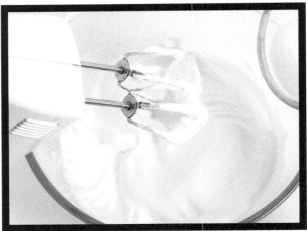

1 **Pre-heat the oven to 140°C/275°F/Gas mark 1**. Line two baking sheets with baking parchment.

Separate the eggs and put the whites into a large, very clean bowl. Add the vinegar to the egg whites and **beat with an electric beater** until the foam becomes very stiff.

2 Add about half the sugar and **continue beating**. Then add the rest of the sugar and **beat until the mixture is thick and glossy** and will stand in stiff peaks.

3 Spoon the meringue into a piping bag fitted with a 1cm (½in) plain nozzle. Pipe about 20 large "mushroom caps" approximately 4cm (1½in) in diameter onto one of the prepared baking sheets, giving them plenty of space to spread. Then pipe about 20 smaller blobs onto the other prepared baking sheet for the "stalks".

4 **Cook in the pre-heated oven** for about one hour until very lightly browned. Wearing oven gloves, **remove the baking sheets from the oven**, place on a heatproof surface and transfer the meringues to a cooling rack with a palette knife. Meanwhile, **melt the butter in a small saucepan, remove from the heat** and place the pan on a heatproof surface. Add the chocolate to the pan and stir until the chocolate has melted completely.

5 **With a knife, level off the top of the meringue "stalks"**, dip each in melted chocolate and attach a stalk to the base of each "cap". Leave in the fridge until cold and completely set.

6 **Heat the milk until hot but not boiling** and add to the remaining chocolate in the saucepan. Stir until the mixture is smooth and well mixed. Dip each mushroom cap into the chocolate mixture to coat. You must do this very carefully to make sure you do not pull the stalks off the caps. Stand the mushrooms on their stalks and leave to dry.

# CHAPTER THREE

# Sweet Treats

# Marzipan Fruit

Makes 225g (8oz) fruit

**YOU WILL NEED**

225g (8oz) white marzipan
red, yellow and green food
  colouring
gravy browning

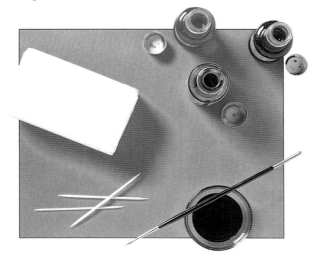

1 On a surface lightly dusted with icing sugar, knead the marzipan well to soften it.

2 Divide the marzipan into four balls.

3 Taking one ball of marzipan at a time, add a few drops of food colouring using a different colour for each ball. You will need one red, one yellow, one green and one orange (mix red and yellow food colouring to make orange).

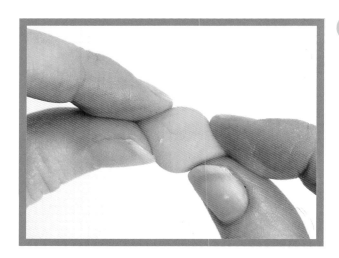

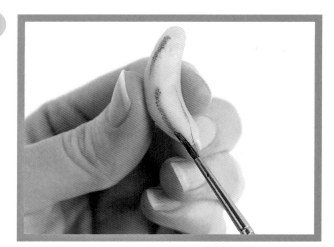

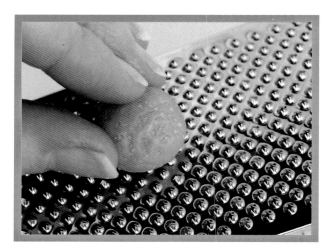

4 Knead the colour into the marzipan until it is well blended and the colour is even. You are now ready to make the fruit.

5 For lemons: roll small pieces of yellow marzipan into lemon shapes and roll over a fine grater to give the surface texture.

6 For bananas: take small pieces of the yellow marzipan and roll into a curved banana shape. Thin the gravy browning with a little water and, using a clean, fine paintbrush, paint lines onto the bananas with the gravy browning.

7 For oranges: make small balls with orange marzipan and roll over a fine grater to give the surface texture. With

a cocktail stick, make a small indentation in the top and put a dot of gravy browning in to indicate a stalk.

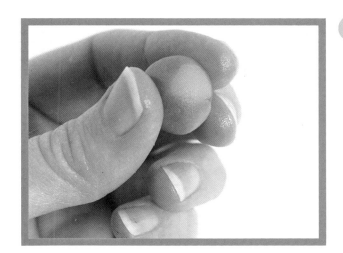

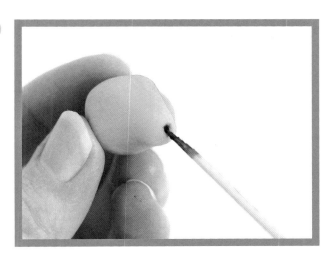

8 For strawberries: mould small pieces of the red marzipan into strawberry shapes. Roll over a fine grater to give the surface texture. Take tiny pieces of green marzipan, flatten into small leaf shapes and press into the base of each strawberry to make leaves.

9 For apples: use red or green marzipan to make small apple shapes. Slightly indent the top of each apple and, with a cocktail stick, put a dot of gravy browning in to indicate a stalk.

10 For pears: take small pieces of green marzipan and mould into pear shapes. With a cocktail stick dipped in gravy browning, make a small indentation in the top of each pear to indicate a stalk.

# St Clement's Creams

Makes about 30

## YOU WILL NEED

1 orange, skin scrubbed clean
1 lemon, skin scrubbed clean
225g (8oz) icing sugar, sifted
4 teaspoons glycerine
about 30 orange and lemon
    jelly segments

1 Finely grate the rind of the orange and put aside in a small dish. Now finely grate the rind of the lemon and put aside in a separate dish.

2 Squeeze the juice from the lemon and put aside. Then squeeze the juice from the orange and put aside in a separate dish.

3 Divide the icing sugar equally between two mixing bowls.

4 Add the lemon rind, 2 teaspoons of lemon juice and 2 teaspoons of glycerine to one bowl and mix well. Now add the orange rind, 2 teaspoons of orange juice and 2 teaspoons of glycerine to the other bowl and mix well.

5 Sprinkle a surface with icing sugar and knead the orange mixture and the lemon mixture separately until each is smooth.

6 Dust a tray and your palms with icing sugar. Using one flavour at a time, pull off small pieces of the mixture and roll into a ball between your palms. Place each ball on the prepared tray.

7 When you have used up all the mixture, press an orange jelly segment (for the orange mixture) or a lemon jelly segment (for the lemon mixture) into each ball and leave for several hours to firm up.

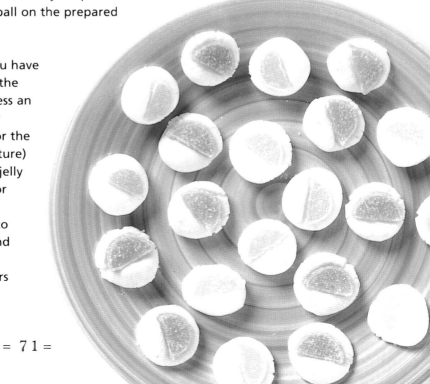

# Honey Fruit Balls

Makes about 20

**YOU WILL NEED**

100g (4oz) ready-to-eat dried dates

100g (4oz) ready-to-eat dried figs

100g (4oz) ready-to-eat dried peaches

1 level tablespoon honey

25g (1oz) sesame seeds

1 Place the fruit on a chopping board and **chop finely**.

2 Put the chopped fruit into a mixing bowl and stir well to combine.

3 Add the honey and mix again.

4 Take heaped teaspoons of the mixture and roll into balls between your palms.

5 Put the sesame seeds into a small dish and roll the fruit balls in the sesame seeds to coat.

**CHEF'S TIP**

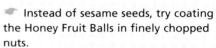 Instead of sesame seeds, try coating the Honey Fruit Balls in finely chopped nuts.

# Coconut Snowballs

Makes about 30

## YOU WILL NEED

225g (8oz) icing sugar, plus
extra for decoration
150g (5oz) sweetened
condensed milk
75g (3oz) dessicated coconut

1 Sieve the icing sugar into a
large bowl.

2 Add the condensed
milk and stir to combine.

3 Add the dessicated
coconut, stir and
then turn out onto
a board. Knead
the mixture until
well combined.

**4**

**5**

**6**

4 Pull off small pieces of the mixture and form into small balls. You can leave these with a coarse, roughed up surface or roll them between your palms to give a smooth surface. Or try a mixture of the two.

5 Sprinkle with a little icing sugar for a snowy effect and leave to firm up on a tray.

6 When firm, arrange the snowballs in small paper cases.

# Crunchy Clusters

Makes about 35

## YOU WILL NEED

50g (2oz) corn flake cereal

50g (2oz) chopped mixed nuts

25g (1oz) currants

12g (½oz) sesame seeds

25g (1oz) unsalted butter, cut into pieces

1 level tablespoon golden syrup

100g (4oz) milk chocolate, broken into small pieces

25g (1oz) hazelnuts, coarsely ground or chopped

1 Put the corn flake cereal into a plastic bag and crush lightly with a rolling pin. Put the crushed cereal, nuts, currants and seeds into a bowl and mix well.

2 **Melt the butter and syrup in a small pan over a gentle heat, stirring occasionally. Remove the pan from the heat** and place on a heatproof surface. Add the chocolate and stir until melted.

3 Add the cereal
mixture to the melted chocolate mixture and stir
until everything is coated in chocolate.

4 Put teaspoons of the mixture into small paper
cases.

5 Sprinkle with ground or chopped hazelnuts and
leave to set.

# Rainbow Lollies

Makes 8

**YOU WILL NEED**

75g (3oz) red boiled
   sweets
75g (3oz) yellow boiled
   sweets
75g (3oz) purple boiled
   sweets
You will also need: extra
   strength foil and eight
   wooden skewers

1 **Pre-heat the oven to 180°C/350°F/Gas mark 4.**
Using a bowl or plate approximately 13cm (5in) in
diameter, mark eight circles in foil and **cut out**.

2 Press the foil circles into patty tins
approximately 10cm (4in) in diameter and run your
finger around the inside bottom rim to indent a
circle in the foil. Make sure the overlap all round is
sticking up.

3 Remove foil cases from patty tins, place on
baking sheets and insert a wooden skewer at the
base of each foil case.

**4**

**5**

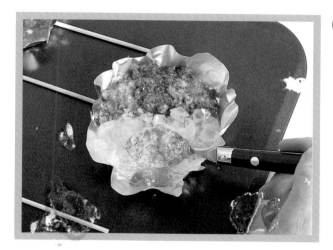

**6**

**7**

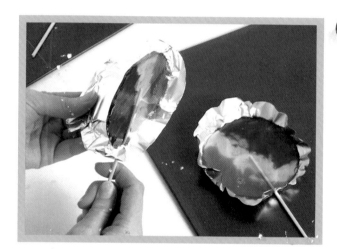

4 Place each group of boiled sweets in a separate plastic bag and **crush with a rolling pin**.

5 Put a thick layer of crushed sweets in each foil case, arranging the different colours in three stripes.

6 **Cook ir the pre-heated oven for about 3 minutes** until the crushed sweets have melted. Wearing oven gloves, **remove the baking sheets**, place on a heatproof surface and leave to cool.

7 When completely cold, peel the foil away from the lollies.

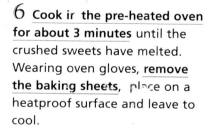

# Jolly Jellies

Makes about 700g (1½lb)

## YOU WILL NEED

1 x 400g (15oz) tin of fruit in juice, eg apricots, cherries, strawberries
450g (1lb) granulated sugar, plus extra for tossing
150ml (5fl oz) very hot water
25g (1oz) powdered gelatine

1 Drain the juice from the fruit, put the juice in a saucepan and the fruit into a bowl.

2 Mash the fruit and then push it through a sieve to make a purée. Add the purée to the juices in the saucepan. You should have about ½ pint of liquid in total. **Warm the fruit liquid but do not let it boil. Remove the pan from the heat**, add the sugar and stir to dissolve.

3 Put the hot water in a cup or small bowl and sprinkle gelatine over it.

4 Stir with a teaspoon until the gelatine has dissolved completely and is no longer gritty. If the gelatine does not dissolve properly, **stand the cup in a saucepan of just boiled water (taken off the heat and placed on a heatproof surface) and stir** until it does dissolve.

5 Add the gelatine mixture to the fruit liquid and stir thoroughly.

6 Pour into an 18cm x 18cm (7in x 7in) shallow tin and leave to cool. Then place in the fridge for several hours to chill and set.

7 When set, dip the base of the tin into a bowl of hot water for a few seconds to loosen. Place a wet plate over the tin and invert the two together so that the jelly falls out onto the plate. **Using a sharp, wet knife, cut into cubes.** Toss in granulated sugar. These should be eaten fairly quickly.

# Crispy Crackles

Makes about 36

## YOU WILL NEED

100g (4oz) marshmallows
25g (1oz) glacé cherries
50g (2oz) puffed rice cereal
25g (1oz) dessicated coconut
25g (1oz) unsalted butter

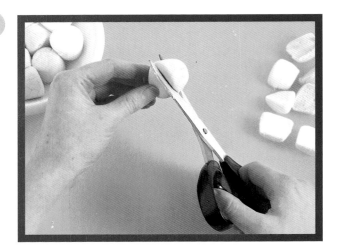

1 Line an 18cm x 18cm (7in x 7in) square tin with foil. If using large marshmallows, **cut them in half using scissors dipped in icing sugar**. Set aside.

2 **Chop the glacé cherries** into small pieces.

3 Put the cherries into a bowl with the puffed rice cereal and coconut and stir to combine.

4 Put the marshmallows and butter into a large saucepan. **Melt the marshmallows and butter over a gentle heat, stirring continuously.**

5 When the marshmallows and butter have just melted, **remove the pan from the heat** and place on a heatproof surface. Stir the cereal mixture into the saucepan and mix well to combine.

6 Put the mixture into the prepared tin and press down with the back of a spoon. Leave to cool and set for two hours.

7 When set, turn out onto a chopping board, remove the foil and **cut the crispy crackles into squares**. Place in small paper cases to serve.

# CHAPTER FOUR

# Perfect Presents

# Mini Florentines

Makes about 18

## YOU WILL NEED

3 level tablespoons golden syrup

25g (1oz) unsalted butter

25g (1oz) light brown soft sugar

25g (1oz) plain flour, sifted

50g (2oz) flaked almonds

25g (1oz) chopped hazelnuts

50g (2oz) glacé cherries, chopped

100g (4oz) plain chocolate drops

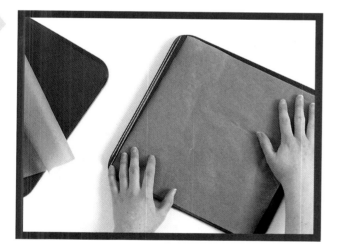

1 **Pre-heat the oven to 180°C/ 350°F/Gas mark 4**. Line two baking sheets with parchment paper.

2 Put the syrup, butter and sugar into a saucepan and **stir over a gentle heat to melt. Remove the pan from the heat** and place on a heatproof surface.

3 Add the flour, nuts and cherries and stir well to combine.

4 Put teaspoons of the mixture onto the parchment-lined baking sheets, leaving plenty of room for spreading.

5 **Cook for 7 minutes in the pre-heated oven until lightly golden.** Wearing oven gloves, **remove the baking sheet from the oven**, place on a heatproof surface and leave the cookies for 10 minutes. With a palette knife, remove the cooked Florentines from the baking sheets and leave to cool on a wire rack.

**CHEF'S TIP**

☞ You can make bigger Florentines. Put larger spoonfuls of the mixture onto the baking sheets and let them cook for a little longer – about nine minutes.

6 Meanwhile, **bring a saucepan of water up to the boil. Remove from the heat** and place on a heatproof surface. Place a bowl over the top of the pan, making sure the water does not touch the bowl. Put the chocolate into the bowl, leave to warm up and then stir until it has melted. Remove the bowl from the pan.

7 With a small palette knife, spread chocolate onto the underneath of each Florentine and place on a wire rack, chocolate side up, to dry.

8 When the chocolate has started to set, mark wavy lines in the chocolate using the prongs of a fork.

# Marvellous Macaroons

Makes about 16

**YOU WILL NEED**
enough rice paper to line two
  baking sheets
2 egg whites, size 3
175g (6oz) icing sugar, sifted
100g (4oz) ground almonds
few drops almond essence
15g (½oz) flaked almonds

1 **Pre-heat the oven to 170°C/325°F/Gas mark 3.**
Line two baking sheets with rice paper.

2 Put the egg whites into a very clean bowl and
**beat with an electric beater until stiff.**

3 Gently but thoroughly fold in the icing sugar,
ground almonds and almond essence with a large
metal spoon.

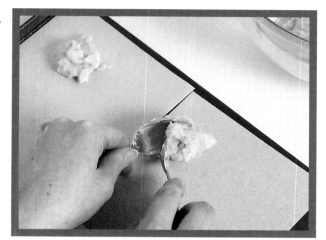

4 Put teaspoons of the mixture onto the baking sheets lined with rice paper, leaving plenty of space for spreading.

5 Place about three pieces of flaked almond in the centre of each macaroon.

6 **Cook in the pre-heated oven for 20-25 minutes** until golden. Wearing oven gloves, **remove the baking sheets from the oven**, place on a heatproof surface and leave until cool enough to handle.

7 **Cut the excess rice paper from the macaroons** and leave on a cooling rack until cold.

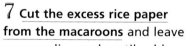

# Vanilla Walnut Fridge Fudge

Makes about 700g (1½lb)

**YOU WILL NEED**

450g (1lb) icing sugar, plus
extra for sprinkling
100g (4oz) unsalted butter
50g (2oz) chopped walnuts
1 teaspoon vanilla essence
3 tablespoons double cream

1 Line an 18cm x 18cm (7in x 7in) tin with foil and
sprinkle with icing sugar.

2 Sift 450g (1lb) icing sugar into a large bowl.

3 **Melt the butter in a saucepan over a gentle
heat.**

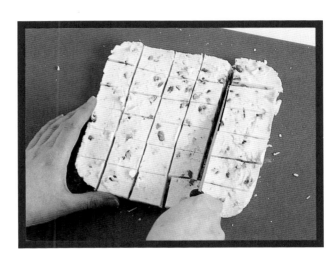

4 Add the melted butter to the icing sugar and stir with a wooden spoon to combine.

5 Add the remaining ingredients and mix thoroughly.

6 Spoon the mixture into the prepared tin and smooth down with a palette knife, pushing the mixture into the corners of the tin. Leave in the fridge for several hours to chill.

7 When set, turn the fudge out of the tin and peel off the foil. **Mark the fudge into squares and cut with a knife.**

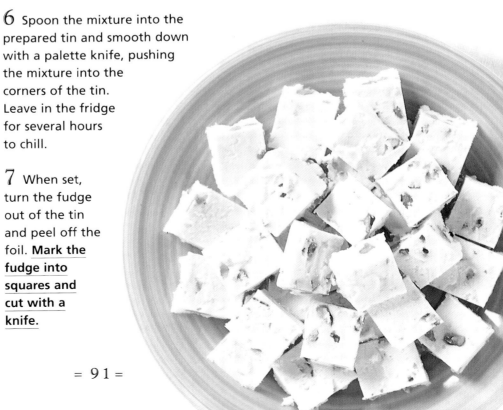

= 91 =

# Minty Melting Moments

Makes about 40

**YOU WILL NEED**

350g (12oz) icing sugar, plus
  extra for kneading
6 teaspoons glycerine
2 teaspoons water
½ teaspoon peppermint
  essence
pink and green food
  colouring

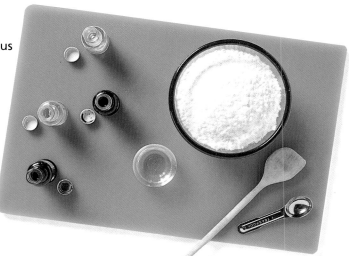

1 Sift the icing sugar into a large bowl.

2 Add the glycerine and 2 teaspoons of water
and mix well.

3 Add the peppermint essence and work into the
mixture. The result should be a stiff paste. Add a
little extra water if necessary.

6 Dust a surface and a rolling pin with icing sugar and roll out each piece of paste separately to a thickness of about 5mm (¼in). Using a small round or decorative aspic cutter, cut the paste into shapes, mark with the prongs of a fork and leave for several hours to firm up.

4 Turn the paste out onto a board sprinkled thickly with icing sugar and knead until smooth.

5 Divide the paste into three and colour ⅓ pink and ⅓ green. Leave ⅓ white.

# Yummy Choc Truffles

Makes about 24 truffles

## YOU WILL NEED

225g (8oz) plain chocolate,
    broken into small pieces
50g (2oz) butter, cut into
    pieces
150ml (5fl oz) double cream
100g (4oz) icing sugar, sifted
25g (1oz) multi-coloured
    sugar strands
25g (1oz) chocolate sugar
    strands

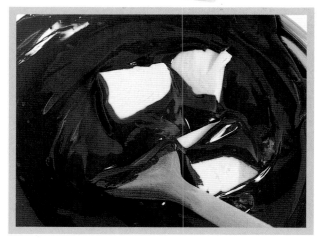

1 **Bring a saucepan of water up to the boil.**
**Remove from the heat** and place on a heatproof
surface. Place a bowl over the top of the pan,
making sure the water does not touch the bowl.
Put the chocolate into the bowl and stir until it has
melted.

2 Add the butter to the bowl and stir to melt.
Remove the bowl from the pan.

3 Add the cream and icing sugar to the bowl and
beat with a wire whisk until the mixture is smooth.
Pour it into a shallow tin and chill in the fridge for
several hours.

$4$ When firm, scrape up teaspoons of the mixture and roll it into balls with your hands. This can get a bit messy, so try to keep your hands cold (so the chocolate does not melt too much) and keep a clean, damp cloth nearby to wipe your hands if necessary.

$5$ Spread the sugar strands on two plates, one for each type. Roll half the chocolate balls in coloured sugar strands and the other half in chocolate sugar strands. Place each truffle in a paper case and then into a pretty presentation box.

**CHEF'S TIP**

☞ Truffles should be kept in the fridge and eaten within four days.

# Measuring Charts

| LIQUID MEASURES | |
|---|---|
| **Metric** | **Imperial** |
| 1.25 ml spoon | ¼ teaspoons |
| 2.5 ml spoon | ½ teaspoon |
| 5 ml spoon | 1 teaspoon |
| 15 ml spoon | 1 tablespoon |
| 25 ml | 1 fl oz |
| 50 ml | 2 fl oz |
| 65 ml | 2½ fl oz |
| 85 ml | 3 fl oz |
| 100 ml | 3½ fl oz |
| 120 ml | 4 fl oz |
| 135 ml | 4½ fl oz |
| 150 ml | ¼ pint (5 fl oz) 8 tablespoons |
| 175 ml | 6 fl oz |
| 200 ml | 7 fl oz (⅓ pint) |
| 250 ml | 8 fl oz (1 US cup) |
| 275 ml | 9 fl oz |
| 300 ml | ½ pint (10 fl oz) |
| 350 ml | 12 fl oz |
| 400 ml | 14 fl oz |
| 450 ml | ¾ pint (15 fl oz) |
| 475 ml | 16 fl oz (2 US cups) |
| 500 ml | 18 fl oz |
| 600 ml | 1 pint (20 fl oz) 2½ US cups |
| 750 ml | 1¼ pints |
| 900 ml | 1½ pints |
| 1 litre | 1¾ pints |
| 1.2 litres | 2 pints |
| 1.25 litres | 2¼ pints |
| 1.5 litres | 2½ pints |
| 1.6 litres | 2¾ pints |
| 1.7 litres | 3 pints |
| 2 litres | 3½ pints |
| 2.25 litres | 4 pints |
| 2.5 litres | 4½ pints |
| 2.75 litres | 5 pints |

| SOLID MEASURES | | | |
|---|---|---|---|
| **Metric** | **Imperial** | **Metric** | **Imperial** |
| 10 g | ¼ oz | 400 g | 14 oz |
| 15 g | ½ oz | 425 g | 15 oz |
| 20 g | ¾ oz | 450 g | 1 lb (16 oz) |
| 25 g | 1 oz | 550 g | 1¼ lb |
| 40 g | 1½ oz | 675 g | 1½ lb |
| 50 g | 2 oz | 900 g | 2 lb |
| 65 g | 2½ oz | 1.25 kg | 2½–2¾ lb |
| 75 g | 3 oz | 1.5 kg | 3–3½ lb |
| 90 g | 3½ oz | 1.75 g | 4–4½ lb |
| 100 g | 4 oz | 2 kg | 4½–4¾ lb |
| 120 g | 4½ oz | 2.25 kg | 5–5¼ lb |
| 150 g | 5 oz | 2.5 kg | 5½–5¾ lb |
| 165 g | 5½ oz | 2.75 kg | 6 lb |
| 175 g | 6 oz | 3 kg | 7 lb |
| 185 g | 6½ oz | 3.5 kg | 8 lb |
| 200 g | 7 oz | 4 kg | 9 lb |
| 225 g | 8 oz | 4.5 kg | 10 lb |
| 250 g | 9 oz | 5 kg | 11 lb |
| 300 g | 10 oz | 5.5 kg | 12 lb |
| 325 g | 11 oz | 6 kg | 13 lb |
| 350 g | 12 oz | 6.5 kg | 14 lb |
| 375 g | 13 oz | 6.75 kg | 15 lb |

| OVEN TEMPERATURES | | |
|---|---|---|
| **Centigrade** | **Fahrenheit** | **Gas** |
| 110° | 225° | ¼ |
| 130° | 250° | ½ |
| 140° | 275° | 1 |
| 150° | 300° | 2 |
| 160° | 325° | 3 |
| 180° | 350° | 4 |
| 190° | 375° | 5 |
| 200° | 400° | 6 |
| 220° | 425° | 7 |
| 230° | 450° | 8 |